Wrong Side of a Fistfight
poems by Ashe Vernon

© 2015 Ashe Vernon

Cover Art: Krystle Adler

1st Edition

All rights reserved. No part of this book may be
reproduced in any form or by any electronic or
mechanical means, including information
storage and retrieval systems, without prior
written permission from the publisher, except for
brief quotations embodied in critical articles and
reviews.

Published in Portland, Oregon,
by Where Are You Press.

*To that beardy kid
(he knows who he is),
thanks.
Maybe not for everything,
but for a whole hell of a lot.*

Table of Contents

I.

HERE IS YOUR ALTAR FOR WORSHIP.......8
SNAPSHOTS...10
THE OPEN FIELD OF MY BODY.............13
STOOP..15
THE POMEGRANATE...........................16
WHY I NEVER ANSWERED YOUR
   TEXTS… ………………………….. 17

II.

YOU……………………………………..20
ROBIN'S EGG HEART(BREAK)………....21
PROFANE...…...22
BAD BOY ICARUS................................24
ON LOVING LOVE..............................26
MISSED CONNECTIONS……………....27
PASS IT OVER THE MOON TO ME.........28

III.

SKELETON SONG...............................31
TROUBLE IS, YOU'RE STILL EXACTLY
THE PERSON WHO I FELL IN LOVE

WITH..33
TO MYSELF, IN MY LAST
RELATIONSHIP...35
THE SEMANTICS OF INFIDELITY...........36
APRICOT WINE...38
BRUISES..39
BURNING BUILDING THEORY..............41

IV.

SURVIVORS GUILT..43
FIELD GUIDE TO LOVING YOURSELF ...45
THE SCIENTIFIC EVOLUTION OF A
PANTHEON OF GODS.......................................46
DEAD DAD POEM..47
OPERATOR..50
REWIND...53
MYSELF, AS A SERIES OF NEWSPAPER
HEADLINES..56

V.

HUCKLEBERRY HONEY......................................60
I DIDN'T SPEAK AT THE FUNERAL.........62
HELLFIRE IN THE KEY OF C..................65
AN OPEN LETTER TO THE EVER AFTER
EPILOGUE IN YOUNG ADULT
LIT...67
POST PANIC ATTACK..70

WINGED SANDALS..............................72
PILLARS OF HERCULES.......................74
KEEPING UP APPREARANCES..............76
WORSHIP IN A BODY BAG....................77
REDEFINING THE CLASSICS................78
OLD WORLD GODS.............................80
CHECKMATE.....................................82
SURVIVAL...84

The sun is giving.
All the time, the sun is giving.
And she's gonna burn out one day.
And it's going to be the biggest,
most terrifying act of self-love
that our little blue world
has ever witnessed.

HERE IS YOUR ALTAR FOR WORSHIP

In East Texas I learned that my body
is less Girl and more Elephant Graveyard.
Here, I am the back pages of a history book;
I am a cathedral of almost-lovers.
Welcome.
I am where you go to abandon your dying.
It'll be like kissing but not as violent.
Come here to bury your dead.
I have always been beast of burden.
Pack animal.
Buy a family plot behind my lungs.
Lay down to rest three generations of
Not Good Enough. You can love me like
a slot machine; here—shove yourself inside
for the chance of getting poetry out of it.
I can be lucky sevens. I can be anything.
I can be the first bar you got drunk in.
I can be a stomping ground for old lovers
who loved only the parts of me they could
put their fingers in—I'll be
the sycamore behind the high school soccer field.
They'll carve their names in me with the stems
of broken wineglasses and call it love.
They can sit in circles and drink fireball whiskey
and brag about how bad I wanted to be touched.
Yeah. I wanted to be touched.
Guess my soda fountain heart was
bad at being a wishing well; all those
copper pennies only ever tasted like blood.

Bodies are supposed to be temples, right?
Well I sure did ransack mine good. In my defense,
marble is marble and stone is stone.
In my defense, no one ever taught me
that I could be holy. In my defense,
wine coolers in Texas summer can taste like
praying if you hold your mouth right.
So I'm the graveyard and not the dead.
Forget this bone business and
just let me live. My body is a temple,
and my gods drink vodka and gin.

SNAPSHOTS

This is a picture of the inside of your chest.
You don't recognize it
because this is not the part of yourself
you stack up against the mirror each morning—
the reflection you turned into a bad punchline
or a political statement—anything
to make it feel less like it belonged to you.
This is the backside of a heartache.
See how simple it is?
Your ribcage never meant to hurt you.
Your windpipe doesn't know how to be pretty,
but she knows how to howl—
and here, I'd like to take a moment
to submit a formal apology to my soft parts
because they kept me warm
when I was trying to freeze to death,
and I hated them for it. An apology
for a starvation that went deeper than my skin.
One for the strongest skeleton I will ever own
and how I kept using the word *girl* against it.
Or how I turned words like *beautiful* into shapes
I could contort myself into. I didn't mean
to compare myself to faces I can't have.
Or spend years trying to carve myself,
like Michelangelo's angels, from the marble—
forgetting what it is to be skin instead of stone.
I let myself be afraid. I was taught to be.
When you learn you are only as good
as your beauty routine, you forget

how to define yourself by anything else.
When all of your value lies
in what you have to offer a man, you learn to be
terrified of them and desperate for them,
all at once; and when fathers tell
of the trenchcoated boogiemen in the bushes,
it is to ensure that they do not raise wolves
instead of Little Red Riding Hoods.
See, the boys who hurt me were only ever
the ones who knew my name.
So fear of the dark was my consolation prize
for being softer than the bruised knuckles
who called themselves boys. Because
when I fashioned myself into a set of teeth,
I was *too violent, too hungry*—
Not. Beautiful. Enough.
To please.
I was a wolf, and they dressed me
in sheepskin
and taught me to fear the foxes,
and I am still afraid.
Because I was the runt of the litter.
So I learned to be pretty on hands and knees;
I learned to be wanted in the dark; I learned
the best way to be less than the sum of my parts.
I learned girls like me don't get happy endings.
But no matter how pretty, the wolf in me
will always be hungry. You can paint the killer red,
and she will still have a taste for blood.
And my lipstick has tasted like metal
for as long as I can remember.

And after a life spent folding myself
into a coffin called pretty,
I finally figured out that I do not have to fit.
This is a picture of the inside of my chest.
You'll notice, it looks a little lived in.
Please forgive the parts of myself I haven't
picked up off the floor yet.
I've been spring cleaning this body since '93.
Still, there is nothing pretty about my aorta,
but these lungs have carried me through a flood.
There is love, here,
in the flex between the vertebrae.
And what I've learned about being pretty,
is I do not belong to it.

It belongs to me.

THE OPEN FIELD OF MY BODY

On the inside, my chest
looks like an open field at dawn:
just peaceful enough for a murder.
Just broad enough to hide a body.
In the river that runs between my lungs,
on the bank beside the
second chamber of my heart,
that's where they
pulled the car from the water.
And how much of myself
had I stuffed in that trunk?
How much had I tried to bury?
I am the serial killer of my body.
I am the religious reformation against
the naked statues of Rome.
I am hacking away at the parts I don't want.
I've been doing it for years.
So far no one has caught me.
I am carving myself into a shape
that no one will recognize
because it is better being the marble
than the monster.
But the beasts in my bones—
they chant my name like a prayer,
like gospel, like a page from a hymnal,
like a war cry, like a riot, like
This is why I am alive, like
This is why I refuse to be silent.
I have taken the knife to the ugly, but

the creatures climb the trees in the darkness.
They are my sword, my armor, my legacy.
They are sharp and wicked and ghastly, but
they are mine; they are mine.
And I will tear myself open
to protect them.

STOOP

The small of my back has seen so much—
my vertebrae are a printing press and I
leave copies of myself in every bed I've ever slept.
This ache is an old one indeed; so I'm sorry
for all the things I made you carry for me.
But no one ever tells you that when
you're picking up your heart, you'd
better be lifting from your knees.

THE POMEGRANATE

In elementary school
I pigeon-holed my skeleton
into any crawlspace I could find
because little girls weren't supposed
to have backbones.
I walked to school with my insides
on the outside—I never unlearned
how to be that raw.
I couldn't fit the bones back
into my body, so with my skull
fitted over my head like a helmet,
I readied my softness for battle.
I was unashamed to be
the flower in the combat zone.
One day I would plunge my fist
into the pomegranate
and dare them to make a victim
of Persephone.
I didn't know that childhood fear
could grow into a rage this mighty,
but I will march with my beating heart
like a beating drum through the marshes.
I will come out on the other side,
and the blood in my mouth will be mine.
I am scouring the badlands of my body.
I am climbing the peaks of the words
used against me. I am painting pictures of
dead men on the palms of my hands, so
there will be no such thing as surrender.

WHY I NEVER ANSWERED YOUR TEXTS

Ever since last summer,
I've kept lonely in every closet in the house.
I don't look in the mirror before
I slip it over my head; I already know
that it brings out my eyes, that
no one would recognize me without it.
Lonely is my favorite dress.

Bluster and I don't know each other well,
but she cheats at cards and
I drive her home when she's had
a few too many—can't count
the number of times
she's drunkenly kissed me.
We don't talk about it in the morning.

Sorrow and I go dancing and
he always forgets his coat, but
no matter how hard we press together
we never seem to keep each other warm.
He always holds me anyway.
He's such a soft, well-meaning thing—

But me, I am a wild-eyed prophet
preaching truck-stop graffiti.
I go to a new city and fall in love
with everyone I meet.
I'll make poetry out of anywhere;
that doesn't try to keep me.

I've done a lot of running away.
Fear and I are childhood friends, and we
get lost on never-ending road trips—
I don't know if I am ever coming back.
I don't know if I know how to.
Our road trip mixtape has two dozen
different songs that all sound like
endings trying to be beginnings,
and we know all the lyrics.

Trouble is, I love better at a distance,
I like people best when they're farthest away,
and that is my narrative tragedy.
But I've never been in love, right?
Or so I keep saying.
And the lie is a noose
I keep hanging myself with.
So I write poems about how this
could all go horribly, horribly wrong
so I won't have to feel guilty
for not going through with it.

You are the softest hurricane of the season,
but there is no room in these ribs
for rain.

YOU

We met on the heels of the lonely.
We were both lost bodies on the breeze,
laced together with promises—
my tongue: a series of fisherman's knots
in the shape of your name.
We crawled out to the place
where the sun does her sleeping:
kissed on the crest of the Earth.
Ten miles from the last place
where Love lay down to rest and
we were too young to know
how to carry a word like that, but
we knew how to catch it: we had
lightning bugs on the tips of our fingers,
just looking for an excuse
to make lanterns of each other. We
chased the sun over the swell of the horizon
until dusk looked like a soft goodnight.
And when the moon clambered up
into the sky behind us, our chests
were full of almosts and you glowed
the color of a heartbeat
and the dark was still and quiet,
and love was a friend of a friend
I didn't know the name of.
But, damn—
I knew just what it looked like.

ROBIN'S EGG HEART(BREAK)

So love didn't taste like you wanted.
So love was all liquor and sweat,
all badly timed apologies,
all bruises on the inside.
So love was uglier than the movies,
hungrier than the stories. So love
took you down to the corner store
at the edge of town and left you in the lot
for the wolves.
So love was rough on you.
It was rough on me too.
I've got a box full of teeth
that are only half mine.
I've got an empty violin case
for a skeleton. Love left me out
in the wilderness, like food for the birds,
and I crawled my way back with their
beaks in my blood, and I made it.
So come here. Let me love
those bruises out of you.
We'll love like children
with a box of bandages—
we won't ask where it hurts.
We'll just kiss all of it. I can't
love the phantom pains all the way better,
but I can love the best way I know how.
I can love you with all that I have.
(I never knew love was so soft until
I knew the soft loving of you.)

PROFANE

The first time he calls you holy,
you laugh it back so hard your sides hurt.
The second time, you
moan gospel around his fingers.
He has always surprised
you into surprising yourself.
He's an angel hiding his halo
behind his back, and
nothing has ever felt so filthy
as plucking the wings from his shoulders—
undressing his softness
one feather at a time.
God, if you're out there,
if you're listening,
he fucks like a seraphim,
and there's no part of scripture
that ever prepared me for his hands—
hands that map a communion
in the cradle of your hips.
Hands that kiss hymns up your sides.
He confesses how long he's looked
for a place to worship and,
oh,
you put him on his knees.
When he sinks to the floor and moans
like he can't help himself, you wonder
if the other angels fell so sweetly.
He says his prayers between your thighs,
and you dig your heels into the base of his spine

until he blushes the color of your filthy tongue.
You will ruin him and he will thank you;
he will say, *please.*
No damnation ever looked as cozy as this,
but you fit over his hips like they
were made for you.
On top of him, you are an ancient god
that only he remembers, and he
offers up his skin.
And you take it.
Once you've taught him how to hold
your throat in one hand
and your heart in the other,
you will have forgotten every other word,
except his name.

BAD-BOY ICARUS

Dear bird-boned boy with the stars in his lungs:
Are they looking? Do they love you?
Do they know how far you've come?
Boy with the sky for a home
who met the dirt like a strong
left hook. Now he wears his clipped feathers
in a noose around his neck because he knows
what it is to be the center of attention
at the hanging.

He knows a grave when
it doesn't look like one.
But who buries the hatchet
and who buries the bodies?
And who says they're not
the same thing these days?

Boy dressed up like a man,
hanging on to the wrong side of hopeful,
plucking butterfly wings because
how dare they; because
once upon a time he
had that kind of softness, too.

He started sleeping with a knife,
when he started sleeping with a gun,
when the bad dreams wore his face
and crowed into his sleep to spit the dead.
They didn't warn him which habits

he wouldn't be able to quit,
and if killing is an addiction, baby,
this is it, this is it, this is it.

So, bird-boned boy—
bad-blooded Icarus boy—
A riddle.
What do you call the monsters
who've made a living off your bones?
By their names, sweetheart.
Can you hear the howling? They've
hitchhiked your hunger, your body—
they're walking the ghost of you home.

ON LOVING LOVE

Love and I swap secrets in
the darkest parts of well-lit rooms.
He's the shiest lover I've ever had—
kisses the lip of his coffee mug,
runs his fingers over everything.
Love is softer than I thought he was.
I always talk of Love with teeth.

But when he sits across the table and
taps his foot against my knee, suddenly
I can't remember why I ever felt that way.
Love is a mess of softness in spring.

He's a weepy drunk—hides his head
in his hands and whimpers
while the world spins. I don't think he's ever
said a cruel word that he actually meant.
Love is so delicate.

We go drinking every week.
We meet at the ugliest bars on the dirtiest streets.
He says there's beauty in the rotten things.
He says the whiskey's good but, god, it stings.

Love chases shots with sweeter things,
but he knows the wicked worst in me.
So we talk a while. And then we trade.
And I am Love.
And he's Afraid.

MISSED CONNECTIONS

You don't read the paper anymore. And
last week the Missed Connections page was
a full-color spread all about your hands—
and how they looked like home in
hummingbird season—I dug it out of your trash
and devoured all this poetry I was never
brave enough to write for you and ached over
how this stranger could write love songs to
every one of your fingers and how those
kinds of words didn't come so easy for me.
When it ended I was left knowing
just how to hold on to you and
none of the ways to tell you I meant it.

PASS IT OVER THE MOON TO ME

When you walk the tightrope
    of redemption, tell the crowd
    to cheer your name for me.
When you make a circus of your heartache,
    tell the moon to look away. Tell her
    it's none of her damn business.
I don't want to know what she thinks
    of forever—she thinks she knows everything.
    But it doesn't count as living if
    you aren't out there living it.
Tell her this day is yours and
    she's not invited to it—tell her
    it's all sunshine from here on out.
When you take the whip to your lonely,
    don't forget how well it knows you.
    You can't carve all the ugly parts
    out of yourself—
    might as well get friendly with them.
    At least for now.
When you leave me
    (which you will)
    you can pack your boxes
    on my side of the bed.
    You can dust the doorknob for fingerprints:
    Yours. Mine. My mother's.
When you leave, you can dig
    through my notebooks until you find
    the page that looks like you.
    You can hate how simple it looks.

28

Never mind that I loved you best.
When you walk the tightrope
    of redemption, know
    that the last standing ovation
    was, is, always from me.
When you kiss the fight right out of me,
    at least I'll have the net at the bottom
    of the highdive left
    to catch me.

I came to kill the king
but wound up kissing him instead.

SKELETON SONG

The dream is always the same.
You crawl out from the dusky nowhere
while I dig the meter of your heartbeat
into the marrow of my bones.
You are a language I am no longer fluent in
but still remember how to read.
In this dream I am everything and I am nothing.
Here and not here.
I am six feet under. I am necromancer.
I bring both of us back from the dead.
In this hand: sacrifice, artifice,
gizzard and pulp and virgin blood.
In this hand: a rickety lineup of
old heartache and spoilt kisses.
They taste like glory in a whiskey bottle.
Our bedroom still smells like witchcraft.
In the dream the stars have never looked brighter,
and we dance on our own graves
while the night wheezes
like an ancient accordion.
We are swallowing crickets whole
just for the chance to feel something
alive in our stomachs.
I kiss the death from your mouth, and it tastes
like moth wings and candlelight; it tastes
like a great migration.
I lick Forever off your neck,
and we invite the moon to dinner.
It's happy hour in a shoddy old dive bar,

but it feels like hunting season;
it feels like loosing the leash on the animal.
You hike up your skirt,
and we fuck under the table,
and there's an old piano hiding in the rafters and
she sings us songs about crossroads and sin.
So we sink our teeth into the heartbeat of evening.
You say, "This is what it means to be alive again."
But there's no dark as deep as the hunger inside
us, and we guzzle the kerosene from the lanterns
so our innards will light—
immolate like a tragedy's silver lining.
Like the burning is something beautiful.
Something bright. In the dream
the fire doesn't hurt, and I watch you
politely undress down to bones:
skin and sinew in a pile by the bedpost.
You kiss me with nothing but teeth.
The pestle and the mortar of you grind
my hipbones into dust.
It is day five hundred and fifty-seven,
and we are still trying to invent new ways
for the same two people
to fall sideways into broken love.
It is day five hundred and fifty-seven,
and I am not haunted by ghosts,
but I sure do dream about them a lot.

TROUBLE IS, YOU'RE STILL EXACTLY
THE PERSON I FELL IN LOVE WITH

I'm sorry you were a coward.
I know how sharp that sounds,
but even now I have dreams where I
slip under your skin; I paint cherry red on my lips
and think of leaving it on your hipbones
like a map of all the ways to leave you breathless.
I think of kissing a concerto of you.
I think of making us breakfast,
but only when I'm lonely.
And that isn't fair to either of us. Still—
I've been having dreams about your mouth lately.
I swear, some of my dreams are innocent,
but I don't wake up crying from the dreams
where you take my clothes off, so I'd rather
talk about those instead.
As much as I wish there wasn't,
there's still some part that's just
a little bit in love and she wants
to road trip up to see you. She's
packaging kisses to send through FedEx.
She forgets the hard parts:
how I was always making room
for all the creaking, clanking aches in you
and smuggling my own out the window.
If this wasn't going to work anyway,
I'm sorry that you're sorry. Because
I would never be this heartsick for a boy
who meant to hurt me, but of course

you did it unwittingly. You're just
a clumsy wrong step in a long line
of blundered feelings, so I'm never going
to be able to hate you for it.
In my dreams you are still so soft.
I would have been happy to love you for it.

TO MYSELF, IN MY LAST RELATIONSHIP

I want you to stop treating hurt like an old friend.
You can't just throw rocks at your heart
and call it romantic;
I know you love him, but he is
too much weight to carry on your back—
only one of you can make it out of here.
All this aching will make a museum of you.
And you will walk through the empty halls
of your chest and see all the things
that loved you half to death. Parents
will tour their children through the wreck
to teach them what it means to light
a body like a match. Trust me when I say
the love isn't worth the price of the flint.
But you love him.
So you love him.
What then?

THE SEMANTICS OF INFIDELITY

The first is a double-dog dare gone wrong. He doesn't touch below the waist, doesn't kiss you on the mouth. He's the good side of a bad joke—talks in promises too big to call friendly. He kissed his mother with that mouth but still won't tell you he loves you, and you carve yourself down to bone trying to fit inside of him.

She is a lighthouse—a cracked whip, a sharp turn. She's a bright white light; she's so fucking alive. And you'd do anything in the book just to get your hands on her.

This one calls you complicated, like it's a compliment instead of the thing that's going to kill you. You are nothing but a body in his bed—all legs, all hands, no head. He talks, he talks, and you kiss him just to make him stop. He is a heartbreak that you pick up and take with you.

You see them together. She is beautiful and you are an open wound. You see them kiss. She is a woman and you are a car accident.

This is a sinking ship dressed in a hallelujah. This is the bed you belong to, and you fall to your knees at the altar of Love, pretending so small a word could ever be enough to save you. Your hips are two hands pressed into an *amen*. Your heart is

36

a killing thing, and you do not know if you are trapped inside or outside it.

You wonder if the line is drawn when you cross it or when you realize that you want to.

APRICOT WINE

The boy in the back room holds the mirror
to his neck. You aren't in love with him.
At least not yet. For now he doesn't know
how to touch you with anything but his hands.
He is a Red Light District in and of himself.
When he offers indulgence like ambrosia,
you lick it from his fingers and he thinks
this is all he knows how to give.
After that the days ferment like apricot wine.
You bite his lips the right kind of russet,
and then at night you dream
of plunging your fist through his ribs
to tear out the songbird inside.
But in the mornings,
you do him violence with
the softest parts of your hands.
We call this surviving. We call this
sin. You'll regret it someday.
But, right now, you aren't in love with him.
Not yet.

BRUISES

I don't write poems about him.
He loved me. That isn't always a good thing.
The road to hell is paved with
hard opinions, sleight-of-hand manipulation,
and phone call, after phone call, after phone call,
after phone call. It wasn't right—
being loved with a leash and a shock collar.
But not every sand trap looks like one, and some
people don't know that they're bottomless pits,
and he had the kind of hands Rome was built on,
so I didn't notice.
Because they weren't throwing hits.
But he spun poison so thick
you'd swear it was honey. Found
a boy like a bad high; I lost days to that one.
Whole years of my life I still define
by the sound of his voice. So he loved me.
And some days that word still looks like
blackmail dressed up pretty.
Never trust the boy who says he'll
kill himself when you leave him.
There aren't bruises for that kind of violence—
no way to take pictures, to say
This is what he did to me.
There was a forest fire in his chest that I
would never have the water to put out,
so I held his hand and I burned with him.
I thought that's what lovers were supposed to do.
Last year I kissed a boy with the same name,

39

and it felt like returning to the scene of a crime:
I was afraid to leave fingerprints. I was afraid
that he would find me—
jump from the throat of a boy whose hands
were nothing like his and demand to know
how I could ever be so heartless as
to abandon him.
He loved me.
That isn't always a good thing.
I don't write poems about him.

BURNING BUILDING THEORY

There was a smokestack pouring
from my window last night
and no one around to see it.
I guess that's what I get for
setting fire to what was left of you,
hoping you'd come
running back for it.

People must think
that being a poet is very slow,
sincere, and quiet.
But at night
the inside of my chest is
so loud,
sometimes I stay awake for days,
trying to out-howl
the hunger
inside it.

SURVIVOR'S GUILT

Imagine you're underwater.
Imagine you've got a tower of hearts—
one stacked on top of the other:
every soft-smile-on-the-subway you ever loved.
So the ocean is six miles deep,
and you've got this lifeline
straight to the surface.
But the catch is,
you have to touch them.
The catch is,
you have to hold that love in your hands
for the first time since the last time
you swore you got over it.

You would drown.

The thing about heartbreak
is it feels too big for your body.
You become cavernous—
a walking Mariana Trench.
Nobody knows how deep you go because
the pressure is heavy enough to fold bodies
into paper cranes and naive enough
to call this beautiful.
All those people who tried
to love the empty out of you,
they didn't know they were kissing
deep sea monsters—that your lips were the lure,

that your hands were the teeth,
that you could blue-ringed octopus
your arms around them and drag them
to the deep.

So you loved more like a pelican eel
than a person. And you're still trying
to outrun the heartache that your heartache
set fire to. But you never wanted
to hurt anyone; and no matter what you
felt for yourself, you will put that fire out
with the oceans on your tongue.
You will put it out if it means
jumping headfirst into the hurricane—
you will do it even if it means a lifetime at sea.
You will do it if it means saving yourself,
even when you had no intention of surviving.

I am ready to go down with the ship,
but I will not take you with me.

A FIELD GUIDE TO LOVING YOURSELF

When you're second choice, you will always
catch yourself wishing that they'd had
the decency not to love you.
Because not being loved doesn't sound
half as bad as not being loved
enough.
So you fashion your heart into a cigar box;
you give it a clasp, a hinge, and a lock.
You package up old loves gone stale.
You haze the room of your heart
with secondhand smoke.
You brag about the ones who almost loved you
like they'd loved you, whatever it takes
to feel beautiful without them.
The love you're aching for looks
like a fourth-story apartment,
like a window with a view,
like a blanket across the back of an armchair,
like candlelight in the living room.
It looks the way Christmas at your mother's
never felt.
It looks like drowning and flying all at once;
it looks like a one-way plane ticket.

It looks like you, darling.
It looks just like you.

THE SCIENTIFIC EVOLUTION
OF A PANTHEON OF GODS

I swear you can see Mount Olympus today.
Out against the seam of the sky,
there's a cloudbank in the shape of every
dream that kept you from sleeping, every
kiss that felt like jumper cables to a car battery,
every bottle of wine that hitchhiked your heart
twenty miles back home through wild country.
And if the Greeks were writing gods, today
Aphrodite would drive FlexFuel.
Hades would buy organic while Zeus
launders money through the accounts
of his "commonwealth" corporation and
Hera fucks his secretary on the side.
They'd give up ambrosia for vodka tonics,
build temples like rest stops on the highways.
Half the myth is word of mouth.
Nothing has ever been written in a stone
too strong to crumble. Everything changes.
These days we've solved mystery with science.
We think we know what the moon's about.
No room for legend and folklore and pretty lying.
But the best place to hide is out in the open,
and I've known mouths that felt like religion, so
who's to say the gods of Olympus
never came down from the mountain?

THE DEAD DAD POEM

I've been waiting for this poem—
I saw the peaks of its skyline more than a year ago,
and I ran.
This is the *I don't wanna talk about it* poem.
The *just got Papa's ashes in my eye* poem.
I wrote my way out of each and every intersection
that could have led me back to his name.
Took three left turns and called it traveling.
I am right back where I started:
I did everything not to get here.
Wrote poems about lovers I never even touched.
I buried myself in ghosts so that I wouldn't have
to shake hands with
yours,
Dad.

We found you cold, Dad.
You were one room over—ten feet away,
dead while I was sleeping,
and I know you didn't mean to,
but I was the last one to see you.
And three a.m. in the doorway to the bathroom
is no way to remember you, Dad.
EMTs stormed the house
like a disaster response team—
covered the place, like cleanup from a hurricane—
nobody told them you took the hurricane
with you when you stopped breathing.
But they knew you went fast. Heart attack, maybe.

No one bothered with an autopsy.
You were so fucking sick, Dad.
Always had been.

They said you went fast, but I lost you so slowly,
over the course of years:
in the cradle of breathing treatments
and pain and pill bottles—
blood tests. Steroids. Insulin.
They say it was quick, but the man who raised me
died a slow and painful death.
I was left with a walking pharmacy
in my father's skin.
I didn't recognize this version of you;
I didn't know how to love him.
He loved me, but he did it like a
Chekhov's gun: loaded threat above
the fireplace. Only he died after Act One,
so the gun never went off. Just stayed
mounted on the wall, a ragged memorial.
A reminder that we'd all survived this.
He wasn't you, Dad.
I hope you'll forgive me
for not missing him.

I just wish those last years
were with someone familiar
instead of tiptoeing around landmines
in the house I grew up in.
I knew you like a child knows a superhero—
I never got you as a person,

48

just as an idol and then
as a handful of napalm.
I was a kid and then I was fuckup,
and you were a bottle of pills
with needles for fingers, who wanted to know
why I didn't come home more often—
I'm sorry.
You were hurting, and I didn't know how
to take care of you. So I hated you
because that was easier than having
a poorly bandaged heartbreak for a father.
But I was only twenty years old when I lost you,
and that's not an excuse.
But maybe it's an explanation.

I took every left turn to keep away
from this poem.
I did everything I could not to write it.
But truth is—
I never wrote poetry until after I lost you.
So I guess that I have you
to thank for it.

OPERATOR

I wonder how many arm's-lengths
you have to be from tragedy
to be a 911 operator.
I wonder if that's the kind of thing
you ever get used to:
if your first week on the job, you go home
and hug your boyfriend a little tighter,
call your mom and tell her you love her.
I wonder if you appreciate people more
when you know what it sounds like
to lose them.
How hard must that be? After all,
how many people have you seen
at rock bottom?
How many stages of denial
have you been made witness to?
How do you do that for a living?

Stay on the line.
Stay calm for me.
Is he conscious?
Is she breathing?
I need you to tell me where you are.
Can you do that for me?

I think every one of us out here
trying to help people just winds up
chasing tragedy: pockets full
of other people's hurting.

Nobody knew what to look for
when I was breaking. Because
I played the Strong Man so many years,
my friends thought the world
would never get too heavy.
So I kept taking calls, forgetting
to phone in my own emergency.
But there was a killer in my body,
and I let it go on killing.
Because that's what you do in a war:
you accept the necessary casualties.

Ma'am, it's okay.
What, exactly, is he doing?
The police are on their way.
Do you know CPR?
I need you to breathe.
Is your mother there?
Is your mother there?
Is your mother there?
The ambulance is coming.

I spent my life playing go-between
for problem and answer
for everyone but me.
When I was drowning, I didn't look
for the surface. I didn't kick my feet.
I reached out. I kissed air into the lungs
of everyone around me.
I didn't know which way was up,
but I knew a hundred different ways

to die for love. I didn't know
there were better ways
to be needed. Because
every good thing I'd ever had
was the kind that bites the hand
that feeds it. So I thought love
looked like teeth instead of tongue.

This is 911.
And the emergency
is that I didn't know there was one.

REWIND
after Patrick Roche

DEAR 15,
When the car breaks down (again), you will reach
deep into your pockets and offer up all of your
measly life's savings to fix it. Your mother will
shake her head, and you will not understand it.
There is a lot you don't understand yet. And
sometimes love comes in the shape of a *no* you
are not equipped to accept. But 15 isn't nearly so
grown up as you think it is and the future is
tottering toward you on shaky legs and it's okay
to be afraid, but here are a couple hints: red meat
makes your stomach hurt, pink is not the enemy,
and girls are really, really pretty. And it's okay if
you want to kiss them.

DEAR 13,
Get a good look at this one—the cherub face,
the voice that rings louder than the one in your
own head; he is the worst thing that ever
happened to you. But it will take four more years
of being crushed into the margins of your own
story to realize that. Right now he comes dressed
as the answer to all of your prayers. But, darling,
if I could go back and keep you away from him,
I wouldn't. He is the atom bomb to your Nevada
body, and he mushroom-clouds everything that
you think you know about yourself to ash.

But he is also one of the only reasons you make it at all. And now he's a rumor of a boy with no home that wants him, and you are still standing. And you are stronger.

DEAR 11,
This is dangerous loving. You are too small, too soft. They are going to make mincemeat of you.

DEAR 17,
You took it too far—turned lonely into solitary confinement and apathy into a pissing contest. But the betrayals don't hurt anymore so, hey, you did it. You let the ones who hurt you go. You let everything go. Your body is a steel wall, ninety degrees of unbending Empty. Your first kiss is a boy you hate; you are done leaving voicemails for a boy who might be dead tomorrow; they are not the same boy, but they might as well be. You will snowball all of this nothing into an avalanche.

DEAR 19,
Please stop, please stop, please stop, please stop. You can't set fire to the hurting.

DEAR NOW (FROM THE REST OF US),
11 wants to know what you did with your hair. 15 misses Dad and 19 doesn't. None of us even recognizes you, and we can't tell if that's a good thing or a bad one, but 13 is in love and 19 is kicking the shit out of her. And 15 is in love and

19 is setting her hair on fire and 17 says she doesn't know what love means anymore. 11 cried her eyes out yesterday and 17 didn't do anything. How did you grow up on the backs of so many broken things? 15 is starving for affection—can't remember the last time she was touched. But 13 still has nightmares about the boy on the bus and the grin on his face and his hand down the front of her jeans and the way her heart felt like a chicken-wire fence caught in a hurricane. 13 didn't get out of bed today. 17 sees the boy and hugs him instead of hitting him and feels sick for weeks but 19 is a survivor and she tells the rest of us to get the fuck over it.

What we mean is…are you happy? We just want 21 to make it. Please just tell us that you're making it.

MYSELF, AS A SERIES
OF NEWSPAPER HEADLINES

Poet on a Livewire, Heavy with Too Many
Tomorrows, Body Made of Copper Plates

Poet 50,000 Watts of Feeling

Poet Eats a Landmine, Starves
to Death Trying Not to Trip It

Poet Flayed Alive, Claims She
"Couldn't Tell the Difference"

Poet Accidentally Swallows
Two Heartbreaks at Breakfast

Poet Overdoses on Hurt,
Tells the Cops It "Wasn't Hers"

Poet Holding "Someone Else's" Depression

Poet Forgets How Heavy the Human Heart Is

Poet Doesn't Write Anymore
but Takes Up Finger Painting

Poet Laughed at Her Own
Reflection This Morning

Poet Laughed with Her Fists, Didn't
Realize Where the Blood Was Going

Poet Wears a Wound Instead of a
Mouth and Kisses Strangers with It

Poet Arrested for "Too Much,
Too Soon," All Over Again

Poet Swallows Salt until She Is
70% Water, 100% Dead Sea

Poet Picks Herself up off the Concrete

Poet Is No Mother but Calls a Stranger "Baby"

Poet Calls Them "God" and "More" and "Holy"

Poet Plays Old Tapes Like She's
Trying to Learn Something

Poet Never Learns

Poet Learns but Does It Anyway

Poet Knows a Hell When She Sees One

Poet's Got a Monopoly on Bad Dreams
but Talks about the Sun Like
Her Whole Body Is Burning

Poet as Celestial Oddity

Poet's Got Stories Made of
Sunbeams and Sprockets

Poet's Gonna Build Tomorrow out
of Duct Tape and Chewing Gum

Poet's Hands Shake but, Damn,
She Sure Knows How to Use 'Em

I am a tiny person
with only two hands.
I am trying to love the world
around decades of war
and skittish heartbeats.
Usually,
I am afraid.
It hasn't been easy,
but I am trying.
I haven't stopped loving yet.

HUCKLEBERRY HONEY

I lost track of myself somewhere in the
rusty cage-fight of growing up.
I just wanted to be heard.
So I put away the tender things
small hands can make and I
cast my bones in lead. Sharpened my tongue
to a razor's edge. I don't recognize the little girl
who put up her fists when this all started.
And I'm still looking for the unmarked grave
where I buried my sweetness: that sugared-honey,
blackberry syrup of me, that reckless loving—
Please.
I just wanna be soft again.
I've got a strong jaw,
but I'm sick of all the swinging—
I didn't use to be like this.
But I was just a stupid kid,
looking to stop the hurting: thirteen when
I coughed up a powderpuff instead of a lung
and mistook the thing for weakness.
I spent the next six years
swallowing splinters and spitting up grenadine.
Came out the backside of nineteen looking like
a gunfight and a fistful of teeth. Hit twenty
like a body on the wrong side of starving,
heart too hungry to eat.
Couldn't keep down all the loving
they tried to feed to me.
I stowed away softness under my bed

so I could pretend I had a suspension bridge
instead of a skeleton. Denial and I
made for very uncomfortable friends.
I sewed up my fractured wishbone like
I could undo breaking a body in half,
but these sutures are splitting at the seams
and I am sick of writing poems
about the ugliness inside me—
I think I made a mess of
this whole growing-up thing.
And I can backtrack through the trenches,
play hopscotch and pick-up-sticks with
landmines and drunken dreams, but
I can't dig up the girl who thought
love would always be a two-way street—
can't distill the honey from the whiskey
'cause there is no honey left in me.
I am a lesson in
Eight Different Ways to Eat Yourself Alive.
You can take the girl out of the center of the ring,
but please,
please,
please.
please—
don't take that little girl outta me.

I DIDN'T SPEAK AT THE FUNERAL

My father was a Man of God.
My father was a liberal,
pot-smoking hippie who cursed like a sailor
and knew two dozen ways to kill a man
with his bare hands—my father was a pastor.
And he had a white-knuckled grip on faith that
I do not fully understand, but
he preached gospel like
he and Jesus were old buddies who
snuck out and went drinking together—
the bail-each-other-out-of-jail kind of friends.
He held hands and broke bread;
he had a way of making a
congregation feel like a family.
He believed in heaven
more surely than I have
ever believed in anything.
My father was just a man.
He had a lot of rage in him.
And when the pills stacked higher
than the pages of a hymnal, he
went looking for god with a spade
and a shovel; he
dug the gospel out of me. Tell me,
what do you call a washed-up preacher
too sick and feeble to do the lord's bidding?
Well, I don't know what you'd call him, but
I called him Dad.
He had a lot of names for me and

one of them was Ungrateful, but
it was hard to be thankful for
the shaking shadow of all the things
my father used to be. See,
my father was a sickness
in a suit of skin. Some days he
was more pain than person, and
he made sure we all knew about it.
I did not grow up in a quiet home.
There was no room for heaven at
the kitchen table; we
had to save a seat for
Pain and one for Loss and
two for all his medications.
They say absence makes the heart
grow fonder, and
my relationship with my father
made a lot more sense
after I lost him.
Death makes a space for forgiveness.
There's lots of space in my parents' house
without him.
I was never on first-name basis with
my dad's idea of god, but for all that
hurting he held in his hands,
my father was a good man.
Even if he was hard to live with.
And he was hard to live with. Dad,
I am still learning how to forgive you.
I'm getting better at it. But you
were an angry, stubborn son-of-a-bitch, and

I guess that runs in the family. And sometimes
it's fucking infuriating to take after someone
you want to be mad at, but
I am my father's daughter. And
I always have been.
And if your god is up there, then
I hope he's playing old blues,
smoking Marlboro Reds—
telling dirty jokes, and singing
hand-me-down gospel with you.

HELLFIRE IN THE KEY OF C

Someone asks, *How are you?*
You say, *Pretty good. Can't complain.*
It's a knee-jerk reaction because it's weird to say,
I just found out I have clinical depression and
I'm trying to make myself care about it.
I'm not complaining about social niceties—
because, god knows, they exist for a reason.
It's just that, some days, they feel like
a bucket of ice water when you've been trying
to send smoke signals, and nobody knows
that they need to look out for you.

To be fair, I'm not very good
at looking out for myself.
And I've found that depression isn't so much
sorrow and anguish as it is existing when
you're not sure you want to. Sometimes
the long, dark tunnel isn't scary or painful.
It just never stops. And you
start to wonder how long the walking lasts.
And hell doesn't look like fire and brimstone.
It looks like nothingness.
I think the souls stuck in hell are
walking a straight line in an empty room
that goes on forever, and they just
don't
care
about it.

When I was a kid, my father said that
hell was a great feast.
And the people at the table
had these long arms with no elbows,
and they were trying to feed themselves—
and they were starving.
He said heaven was a great feast, too.
He said the people at the table
had these long arms with no elbows,
and they were feeding each other—
and they were full.
I think this was supposed to be
a story about selfishness. Or about
how hell is self-inflicted, but I think
it's a story of short-sightedness. I think
it's about how circumstances do not define us,
but we've got to look past our elbowless arms,
or we're going to keep starving
our way through this.

The metaphor does nothing for what I'm feeling.
Because depression is chemical.
Poetry makes for pretty Band-Aids,
but it Does Not Heal All Wounds.
That's okay.
I like my pretty bandages—
show them off like children on the playground:
This is where I broke my heart,
and this is where it almost broke me back,
but listen—don't these similes
look good on me?

66

AN OPEN LETTER TO THE
HAPPILY-EVER-AFTER EPILOGUE
IN YOUNG ADULT LIT

What the fuck is this?
What am I supposed to do with this?
So our hero grows up,
marries his high school sweetheart,
has two-point-five kids,
and that's it?
That's your fairytale ending?
Hold on.
Let me get this straight.
I'm living in an economy that looks
like the backside of a hangover,
and I'm supposed to resonate with this?

Your White Picket Fence narrative
is an outdated flavor of success:
comfortable, middle-class complacency
that is a stranger to me. I don't know
what this looks like. I didn't even see it
in my parents.
The American Dream isn't an option.
I don't even want it.
I wouldn't know what to do with it
if you dropped it in my lap.

Do I look like I have time for two
snot-nosed kids orbiting my nuclear family?
I'm working two jobs to pay rent.

And then there's the high-school-sweetheart thing,
because really? Gross.
I wouldn't even let my high school friends
watch my dog much less raise my children.
Did any of these young adult fiction writers
actually go to high school?
I'm not marrying anybody from that.
And don't think I haven't noticed
that all these authors are from
two generations back.
You aren't "hip," sweetheart.
You aren't speakin' my language.

We're not living out your teenaged wet-dreams.
We are hearts carved into the shape of fear,
standing on the precipice between
complacence and revolution,
and all it will take is a single step.

I'm not looking for the kind of love
that lasts forever. I'm begging for scraps.
Because I know, eventually,
I'll want to take that job in Chicago.
And he's going to want to stay close to his mom,
or she'll want to start that new business,
and we'll be so busy paying bills we'll forget
to kiss goodbye in the morning, and love
will go back to being a story I tell only
when I'm lonely. Which these days
is all the time.

I'm not buying your Happily Ever After
because you're preaching to a choir
that would be content with so much as
a Happily Till Tomorrow.
Don't take me on the most fantastic adventure
of my life and then end it in something so
unattainable and ordinary.
Don't give me a character that looks like me
and then give her a life like my grandmother's.
I'm trying to survive here.
I don't need Happily Ever.
I'm just looking for an After.

POST–PANIC ATTACK

First,
quit picking old wounds
and going for walks in the aches
and pains you already made it through—
you call it healing, but
it sounds like a good way
to take a haunting home with you.
LONELY is a no-vacancies sign
for an empty room on the backside
of your chest, and there will never
be enough people to
love that empty out of you.
Love will not save you.
You will save you.

Remember,
no matter how much you need
a voice at other end of the line
who only wants to take care of you,
it is a felony to call 911 just because
you need someone to talk to.
You cannot shrink to radio static,
to heavy-breath on a telephone.
Your aching does not end
in an ambulance.

Now, breathe.
Yes, I know you've heard this one before.
Do it anyway. Got ribs like

the wrong side of a fistfight, yeah?
That's from the hyperventilating.
Your lungs just survived a
car crash inside your body.
Be gentle with them, please.

Find the pocket of your heartbeat
where you keep Forgiveness.
We will try again tomorrow—
I know you've got a bone to pick
with tomorrow, but it's coming anyway.
Listen, in a few hours
our little world will
turn herself right-side-up again,
and you will forget about
all the ways this lonely night
sang you watered-down blues and
your hands will start to make sense again.

You think you've seen every ugly corner
of this whole rotten world, but listen:
There is an infinite number
of things we don't know and,
statistically speaking,
at least half of them
are probably
very, very beautiful.

WINGED SANDALS

My generation is muddied royalty,
like diamonds in a coal mine.
They dragged us through the dirt,
used our names as scandal.
They said we couldn't, but we
are the gods of the subway—
Dionysus in skinny jeans—
Nemesis in a studio apartment—
Hephaestus with his grandmother's ashes.
We may not be sacred anymore,
but we remember Mount Olympus.
When the kingdom of heaven fell, we
were built from the leftover stratus.
Call me whatever you want, but I have
crossed the river Styx with the world
on my shoulders.
Tonight I am Athena with
my keys between my fingers.
When Apollo drags the sun into the sky,
I will follow on foot—
thousands of years, into the maw of the leviathan,
past the fall of Rome, past the birth of civilization.
I will walk backward into the Big Bang
and take my dark matter with me.
Because when you force two thousand years
into the skin of one girl, she learns
how to tear down the garden wall
and grow her roots into the city.
I left home and took the fall of Troy with me.

I am the patron saint of my own survival, and
I have sacrificed everything
except my own heartbeat.
And I didn't last a thousand years
not to go down swinging.
My generation is the echo of the mountain.
The gates of the Underworld
come crashing at our feet.
I am starving for a fight, and I've got
winged sandals to steady me.

PILLARS OF HERCULES

Hold that heavy heart high, my boy.
You are no Atlas, but the head on your shoulders
gets harder to carry every year.
So you fashion your left hand into a guillotine
and your right into a noose
and wait to see which your neck takes to first.
I've seen those ribs go on for miles, but
your mouth still feels like a steel trap and
you keep quiet for fear of letting the cold in.
Or letting it out.
You can't keep track anymore.
So life is a game of Russian roulette,
and you keep loading rounds in the chamber
because your papa always taught you
how to hedge your bets, and
Dead Men Pay No Taxes.
Nobody said it would be easy, but damn—
it would have been nice to have a little warning.
And far be it from you to make broad, sweeping
statements of morality, but there's something
about the system that's always seemed flawed.
But love was a language or an algorithm
you couldn't wrap your mouth around—
missed equations, conjugations.
For years they told you
god put your heart in upside-down.
But you always knew how to touch; it's just
that nobody ever touched you better than the way
you touched yourself.

And there are all these people calling orgasm
some kind of miracle, so I guess that makes you
holy man:
messiah in your own temple.
If love comes in too many colors, you
were a kaleidoscope printed in sepia
and no one ever bothered to see the beauty in you.
The media was selling sex, so
you met them at the auction house.
Counter Offer: Love isn't for everyone.
I can find a body beautiful
without wanting to be inside of one.
Counter Offer: Self-made miracle, working in the
corner of a darkroom,
developing like a photograph,
along with all the ways nobody knows
that you like
to be touched.
Counter Offer: Alone, Not Lonely.
We've all got our burdens, but this
has never been one.

KEEPING UP APPEARANCES

Where I'm from we don't talk about
the burning things. The polite thing to do is not to
sneeze when the smoke seems all encompassing.
We've all got arson in the drywall, sugar.
That's what it means
to grow up Straight-Laced South.
That's real Southern Comfort. I've never known
a family tree that wasn't a little bit crooked;
we just don't talk about it here.
Everything is okay. Even if
the roof leaks communion wine. Here,
gospel's so stiff it could stand up
and walk on its own. Here, the Heat
has a room in every household and he
makes for a miserable host.
Got planation homes held up with
four generations of bent shoulders.
Here, I have seen women shrink
themselves down to communion wafers:
bland and palatable, to be eaten in one bite.
There's a fire in the coat closet, and it smells
like skipping Sunday in the Bible Belt—
it smells like eating your family whole
so you can tell the world all the ways
you miss them.
We don't talk about the smoke here.
But we sure love to brag
about all the ways we survived
Southern Livin'.

WORSHIP IN A BODY BAG

In deep East Texas,
two houses of worship reign supreme:
god and methamphetamine.
They do not share a congregation.
Usually.

There were a lot of dealers
in my old apartment complex.
The cops came every other week.
Once they flushed out the apartment
right underneath me.

Nobody talks about these things.
It's a reality of small-town Bible Belt that
there are the ones who do the praying
and there are the ones who see
the face of god.

And they are not the same.

REDEFINING THE CLASSICS
after "I Am Not the Sea" by Lora Mathis

I never liked English class
because I had to listen
to men do me violence in classic literature.
You learn quick in a landscape of
Gatsbys and Heathcliffs,
Ahabs and Tom Sawyers—
that the only story worth reading is man's.
Only rough-knuckled young boys
have adventures, and soul searching is reserved
for white-bearded alcoholics and
their foolhardy protagonists.
Never mind what the women did.
I got sick of the legacy of violent men,
the broken-record history of heartsick girls
waiting to be kissed, like that's all we're good for.
So the prodigal son returns—
yeah, well his sister never left.
While Hemmingway and Kerouac were off
taking the world by the neck of a bottle,
we were trying to keep the damn thing together.
I don't believe that women went quietly
into the sidelines of history.
So the great women, the few women,
of classic literature find themselves with
daggers in their hearts,
scarlet letters on their skin.
We walk, open armed, into the mouth of the sea.
We crawl into the wallpaper and never come back.

We are tragedies, if we are anything.
And here we are, teaching the same tired books
they've used in the classroom for years,
creating next-generation nihilist narcissists:
men longing for the kind of thick,
underbelly-sludge of the earth
that the beat poets waxed prettily about—
Keep me away from the boys who love Bukowski.
I love myself too much.
I will not be turned into a clever piece of rhetoric,
another example of why
"women can't be trusted."
I will not beat myself into the bottom of a bottle.
I don't want to be poetry if it means first
being a punching bag. This is for the
prodigal daughters who found themselves
without scouring the earth for it.
For the women who shook the country to
its foundations and still found time
to raise their children. This is for
the ones they burned at the stake
for daring to take chances.
They wrote us as witches,
but speaking up against it
is the only magic I've ever
been willing
to burn for.
So come and get me.

OLD WORLD GODS

You gave up on love six generations back,
but when she slips her hands under your skirt
you remember what it is to feel holy again.
When the world forgot your name, she
moaned it into your mouth; she
carved it into your skin with the knife
you gave her back when
you were still young and violent—when the men
who worshiped at your temples came with
blood and wine and sacrifices. And
for all the years in abject silence, you both
can remember the high of the hunt
and the sound of the sirens. So you
get drunk on whiskey and drunk off each other
and swallow whole the parts of the city that
no one else touches. You have never
been afraid to crawl through the gutter. Holding
hands on the outskirts, digging through sin:
cheap shots, body shots, head shots.
She pins you to hotel doors—
not a goddess anymore,
but she still looks like religion in high heels.
She kisses you godless. Whispers,
We dress like princesses to go out and kill kings.
You are each the other's own personal monster,
and you let yourselves both off the leash.
Feral teeth made for killing, for mauling,
for kissing: she's in love
and you don't remember the word, but

you know what it is to be inches inside her,
to want to give her the world,
and give it to her bleeding.
And this is your Church of Broken Necks,
of Missed Rent, of Bad Habits.
So you're not gods anymore—
but you can burn down the city
and still be some kind of messiah
and you can do it,
so long as you're burning beside her.
So long as it means even the echo of a chance
to feel just on the wrong side
of holy.

CHECKMATE

They called you soft. They called you trembling.
You raise your arms and they see you
featherweight in the face of the world.
Girl thing. Too porcelain for
rough-knuckled boxing, too china plate
to take a punch and stay standing.
They saw your liquor and your lace and
called you high society: nothing more
than ceramic smiles with painted teeth,
heart nestled in lipstick-kissed shot glasses,
designer dresses on bedroom floors;
they came with knives and forks.
They saw no insurrection inside you.
But you took the whetstone to every curve—
turned "woman" to a prayer when
they used it like a curse.
You wore your girlhood as a dagger
on your sleeve—small and pink
and pretty. No one sees the violence
in the beautiful things.
You learned that the right kind of softness
was enough to unravel kings.
So you were soft. You were trembling.
You were girl in all the ways
that made you gentle;
woman in all the ways
that made you wise.
You black widow spidered the ones
who thought they had a right to keep you—

not made for being put on display.
Beautiful, not like a dusty work of art.
Beautiful like a wild thing:
overgrown and feral.
Beautiful like a drumbeat.
You leaned into the howling
of your own body. Met fire with fire—
you burned and you burned
until skin was all smolder.
Sinner they named you,
so sinner you became:
Hungry and heavy
you sharpened your teeth.
If this is a war, you don't know if you're winning,
but you'll carry your soft parts like weapons.
If this is a fistfight, you've never thrown punches,
but your knuckles are bleeding
and your mouth is a bruise.
But if they think this is bad,
they should see the ones
who did this
to you.

SURVIVAL

This is the first trumpet to sound
in an empty concert hall. It's rain against
a window that's always let a little water in.
This is for the words you wished you could
pull back inside you but, more than that,
it's for the words you never let out.

.

This is a story of survival.
It is your story,
even when you feel like that word
does not belong to you.

.

This is a love song for your clumsy heart
and all the times it sank into arms
that were too small for it.
For the mornings when getting out of bed
was the hardest thing you did all day,
this is a ballad of frightened breaths
in a mason jar on the bedside table.

.

I know—
You are not trying to move mountains.
You are not trying
to brush shoulders with the universe. All you want
is enough room in your own chest for
a pair of lungs that haven't felt like yours in years.

.

So this is a reminder
that—aside from everything else—

you are still here,
and you are still breathing.
And maybe you don't always want to be.
And that's what makes everything you are
so brave.

.

You have a small ocean inside of you;
you have the breath of a country in your lungs;
your heart beats in time to the turn of the planet,
and you
are a force of nature
simply for making this far.

.

This is an *I love you.*
This is tucking you in at night.
This is a drumbeat,
welcoming you home from war.
You are a white-knuckled miracle.
And you don't have to fight anymore.

86

ACKNOWLEDGMENTS

Thank you to the *Rising Phoenix Review* for first publishing "I Didn't Speak at the Funeral."

To the family who has always, always supported me. Thanks for not wanting me to be a doctor. Or for not mentioning that you wanted me to be a doctor, if you did.

To Write About Now for practically raising me and changing everything I thought I knew about poetry.

To Caitlyn Siehl—without you, I would have never had the guts to put my work online. I would never have made it here. I owe you the world, but that's not in the budget so here's a big chunk of my heart instead.

To Bill Moran, for being the driving force behind getting my poetry on its feet. There would have been no tour without you.

To Jordan Hamilton, I wish I knew what to say. I wish I knew how to thank you. I wish there were enough words for it. You're gonna take this whole fucking world by storm, kid.

ABOUT THE AUTHOR

Ashe is a poet, an actor, and a playwright. Her first book, *Belly of the Beast,* was published in November 2014 by Words Dance Publishing. Since then she's graduated from college and stumbled her way onto stages across the country. At 5'2", Ashe is a very tiny person with very tiny hands and a whole lot to say about it.

ALSO AVAILABLE FROM
WHERE ARE YOU PRESS:

This Is How We Find Each Other
By Fortesa Latifi

Healing Old Wounds With New Stitches
By Meggie Royer

You Can Do Better
By Alex Dang

It Looked A Lot Like Love,
Kristina Haynes

The Women Widowed To Themselves
Lora Mathis

Until I Learned What It Meant
Yena Sharma Purmasir

Where Are You Press is a publishing house
founded in 2013 in Portland, Oregon. We create
small, beautiful books of poetry and prose
highlighting the voices of women and people of
color.

For more visit our website at
www.whereareyoupressstore.com